Little Laureates

Grampian

Edited by Angela Fairbrace

First published in Great Britain in 2007 by:
Young Writers
Remus House
Coltsfoot Drive
Peterborough
PE2 9JX
Telephone: 01733 890066
Website: www.youngwriters.co.uk

SB ISBN 978-1 84602 993 6

Foreword

Young Writers was established in 1991 and has been passionately devoted to the promotion of reading and writing in children and young adults ever since. The quest continues today. Young Writers remains as committed to the nurturing of poetic and literary talent as ever.

This year's Young Writers competition has proven as vibrant and dynamic as ever and we are delighted to present a showcase of the best poetry from across the UK and in some cases overseas. Each poem has been selected from a wealth of *Little Laureates* entries before ultimately being published in this, our sixteenth primary school poetry series.

Once again, we have been supremely impressed by the overall quality of the entries we have received. The imagination, energy and creativity which has gone into each young writer's entry made choosing the poems a challenging and often difficult but ultimately hugely rewarding task - the general high standard of the work submitted ensured this opportunity to bring their poetry to a larger appreciative audience.

We sincerely hope you are pleased with this final collection and that you will enjoy *Little Laureates Grampian* for many years to come.

Contents

Old Rayne Primary School

Pitmedden School

Tough Primary School

The Poems

The Seasons

Spring creeps over the Earth,
She warms up plants, cold from Winter,
Flowers peek through the soil, shy.
They dress in bright colours,
Spring cheers up sad skies.

Summer storms into the year,
Angry at being second to decorate the planet,
He throws yellow and gold ribbons at us, teasing,
Crops curl up and die from beneath his fiery glare.
Summer feels savage.

Autumn waves at us from behind September,
Eager to please.
Plants and trees go all out to welcome him,
Showing off in copper and gold.
Autumn takes his hold.

Winter arrives to greet the Earth,
Pillow-fighting with Autumn.
Watching feathers float down, faster and faster,
Winter brings delight.
But she has an evil side.
Water drips that annoy her, she turns to icy daggers,
But Winter just laughs as she dances in the cold.

Eilidh Johnston (12)
Arduthie Primary School

Snowfall

The snow falls noiselessly, dancing in the night,
Spinning through the sky ever so light,
Coating houses in a blanket of white,
Lying there, what a beautiful sight.

It sparkles silently falling in sheets,
Sheep look up and start to bleat.
Hour after hour it lays a thicker blanket.

The snow falls noiselessly, dancing in the night,
Spinning through the sky ever so light.

Emily Esson (11)
Arduthie Primary School

Lightning!

Lightning reaches its destination
searching desperately for victims.

Lightning strikes trees with all its force
sends people yelling, roaring and dashing for shelter

Lightning violently takes snapshots
of our frustrated faces.

Lightning attempts to pierce its prey
raids cities like thieves on a rampage.

Lightning tires;
dies.

Josh Halliday (11)
Arduthie Primary School

Blizzard The Bully!

Blizzard arrives to bully the town!
It freezes and cracks
It's sore to the face when it's hard and icy
The flakes grow like a young child growing into an adult
A complete whiteout causes havoc on roads
Then calmly losing its powers as it is blown away
Then it's gone
To leave a white town and a quiet town.

Josh Leary (11)
Arduthie Primary School

Acid Rain!

Acid rain tumbles from its cloud,
Its aggressive body seeks its prey,
Acid rain charges down to our harvest crops,
making uncontrolled fires.
Acid rain murders for fun and games,
creates puddles of deadly sins.
Acid rain thinks it is supreme,
by using its muscles to squeeze out pain.
Acid rain speeds down to Earth,
making craters in the roads.
Acid rain sluggishly passes,
leaving havoc behind.
Then as it reaches its end it dies.

Callum Edgar (11)
Arduthie Primary School

The Rain

Rain clouds tiptoe across the sky,
Turns off sun's light.

Rain threatens people,
Pushes them inside.

Rain murders holidays,
Smothers the town in pools of water.

Rain drowns animals,
Floods roads, rivers and basements.

Rain dances on the rooftops,
Runs down gutters.

Rain slowly stops,
Sun peeks through the clouds,
Sun brightens the sky.

Lauren Hay (11)
Arduthie Primary School

Wind

Wind rallies on, the breeze turns to a gale.

Wind turns off the light,
Darker and darker so that no one sees.

Wind thrashes garden sheds,
Rattles them and they rattle back.

Wind chases its victims,
Pushes them into shelters.

Wind kicks buildings,
Thrusts them into the darkness.

Wind huffs,
Wind dies.

Ruth Williams (12)
Arduthie Primary School

Breeze

Breeze emerges,
Breeze's chilling fingers tickle people's bones,
As she plays her favourite game.

Breeze sings as trees and bushes dance to her swirling rhythm.

Breeze tumbles down dark alleyways, sweeping away fallen leaves.

Breeze cools down and dries out people's washing.

Finally,
Worn out,
She collapses.

Hannah Woodfin (12)
Arduthie Primary School

The Alphabet

A is for apple, shiny and red,
B is for baby, tucked up in bed.
C is for cake, tasty and sweet,
D is for duck, my favourite meat!
E is for elephant, so tall and so fat,
F is for fajita, so round and so flat.
G is for grannies, who spoil you a lot,
H is for hat, that's what I've got.
I is for igloo, made out of ice,
J is for jelly, *mmm* that tastes nice!
K is for kite, high up in the sky,
L is for lamb, goes nice in a pie.
M is for mop, clean up the floor,
N is for noise, please shut the door!
O is for octopus, lives under the sea,
P is for postman, coming to me.
Q is for queen, regal and rich,
R is for rugby, played on a pitch.
S is for sunshine, happy and bright,
T is for torch, let's have some light!
U is for umbrella, here comes the rain,
V is for vegetables, good for your brain.
W is for wildlife, here comes Bill Oddie,
X is for X-ray, takes shots of your body.
Y is for yoghurt, 100 per cent dairy,
Z is for zoo, the lions are scary!

That is my alphabet, as you can see,
Thank you for listening, it was made up by me!

Jack Mercer (11)
Arduthie Primary School

Scarecrow

Standing there all proud and tall,
Soon to flop down ready to fall.

Farmer comes each day,
To check that you scare the birds away.

Standing there in ragged clothes,
Your purpose is to scare off the crows.

Winter comes and they take you down,
Cold and tired and your clothes all brown.

Spring arrives here again,
Along with the lambs, the chicks and the hens.

You're put back up to stand there tall,
It's a new start so you will not fall.

Hannah Mitchell (11)
Arduthie Primary School

The Devil Dog Duke

Glaring red eyes in a devil stare
Ears like horns, alert and scary.
Like a lion he stalks his prey
Waiting for one to fall stray.
As tall as a horse with powerful legs,
He jumps on your back with claws like knives.
Teeth like a shark's he rips you apart,
Nothing is safe from his grasp!

Ross Curley (11)
Arduthie Primary School

Rain

Grey clouds sit there in the sky,
Doing nothing,
It's all quiet,
Until . . .
It starts showering down with rain
And then it lashes on the people and houses
Streets start to flood
Rain slowly dies
Down.

Jack Maxwell (11)
Arduthie Primary School

Rain

Stuck inside on this rainy day,
Oh, how I wish I could go out to play!
I would happily put my wellies on
And not get too wet if I can.
But sometimes on a rainy day,
You can't beat knitting with your gran!

Joanne Carstairs (11)
Arduthie Primary School

Clothes

Dirty clothes go in the basket
Clean ones go in the drawer
But since I can't be bothered
I throw them all over the floor.

Ross Hodgkinson (11)
Arduthie Primary School

My Sister Is So Evil

My sister is so evil
She pours paint down the stairs
She throws rocks through windows
And pulls out people's hairs

My sister is so evil
She's so easy to spot
She walks around with pale white skin
And trousers that she thinks make her look hot

My sister is so evil
But when the day is out
She slumbers quietly
Without a single shout
But before she goes to bed
She remembers to do one thing
She always sets a booby trap
For the postman and
The letters that he brings

My sister is so evil
Of that you must agree
But I cannot really moan at her
Because she learnt it all from me!

Connor Mackie (11)
Arduthie Primary School

Storm

Thunder awakes,
Shouting from the sky,
Roaring with wrath.

Lightning joins in,
Flashing brightly at the trees.

Rain throws itself down,
Tapping on the tattered bins.

The storm rages,
Thrashing its muscly arms.

Trashing plants,
Lightning destroys them,
Taking them to their bitter death.

Fearsome wind batters through the trees,
Stripping them bare.

Leaving its winnings,
The storm creeps away
An evil smirk on its face.

Samuel Howard (11)
Arduthie Primary School

One Little Piggy

One little piggy went to town
He saw some pork and he did frown,
'How can people be so cruel?
It just really isn't cool.'

Piggy then went to get some food
And found the shops were all so crude,
'Where is all the tasty swill?
All this junk makes me feel ill.'

Along came a businessman with food galore
And took little piggy to his factory door,
Piggy knew no more about this, why?
Because he ended up in a pork pie!'

Robbie Western (12)
Arduthie Primary School

There Once Was A Boy Called Scott

There once was a boy called Scott
Who picked his nose a lot
He went to bed
And bumped his head
And out came a whole lot of snot.

Calum Hay (11)
Arduthie Primary School

Up, Up And Away

I watch everyone gliding,
Spiralling, twisting, turning, soaring, swooping,
I wanted to try
I jumped, I fell, hurtling to the ground
Like a very heavy stone,
I lay on the ground dazed and sore,
I got up and ruffled my soft, fluffy feathers,
I tried again, I jumped, I fell down, down
Then I found myself soaring,
The strong wind beating against my chest,
I soared high over treetops and glided to the ground
Landing on a rough tree branch.

Holly Allan (9)
Ashley Road School

Tell Me If You Like . . .

Tell me if you like . . .
falling off a ski lift.

Tell me if you like . . .
reading a comic on the toilet.

Tell me if you like . . .
throwing away bad school reports.

Tell me if you like . . .
staring at teachers.

Tell me if you like . . .
your mum kissing your feet.

Tell me if you like . . .
blocking ant holes so the ants go mad.

Tell me if you like . . .
singing last year's Christmas hymn.

Thomas Rowbotham (9)
Ashley Road School

In One Second I Can . . .

In one second I can . . .
see my magical dream come to an end, a sad end,
like the white turtle dove who had been soaring the waterfall
and rainbow for hours and finally landing.

In one second I can . . .
taste the scrummy lemon cake
but then it is all gone,
making me want to eat more.

In one second I can . . .
feel the furry bark rush across my hand,
then again and again.

In one second I can . . .
smell the burning ash of the barbecue
threatening my nose and face.

In one second I can . . .
hear a man falling overboard *splash!*
and people running to get him!

Eilidh Matheson (9)
Ashley Road School

Shhh

Shhh! What's all that noise?
It's not easy being a leaf you know.
First you have to make your way out
Of the bud all by yourself.
You're always changing colour.
Then there's the 20-foot fall from grace.
Oh I wish I was an evergreen.
Finally you get stood on and run over.
So *shhh,* please keep it down.

Brooke Feeney (9)
Ashley Road School

Tell Me If You Like . . .

Tell me if you like . . .
when a job is done when you don't even realise!

Tell me if you like . . .
farting right next to your mum!

Tell me if you like . . .
to score a goal!

Jamie Buglass (9)
Ashley Road School

Tell Me If You Like . . .

Anything in the whole entire galaxy.

To pretend there's aliens attacking the world
and you are helping to stop them.

To lie in your bed on a school day
until your mum or dad goes mad.

William Van Wachem (9)
Ashley Road School

Tell Me If You Like . . .

Tell me if you like . . .
drinking lemonade
and then you feel bubbles up your nose.

Tell me if you like . . .
jumping as high as you can
on your trampoline and thinking you can fly.

Mixing your food up and making it into a farm.
Tell me if you like!

Grace Flett (9)
Ashley Road School

Tell Me If You Like . . .

Tell me if you like . . .
watching your gerbil or hamster
doing the monkey bars on the top of your cage.

Tell me if you like . . .
Waking up at a friend's house
and having no idea where you are.

Tell me if you like . . .
waking up on Saturday
and smelling sausages and eggs in the morning.

David Finlayson (9)
Ashley Road School

Tell Me If You Like . . .

Throwing rocks into the sea
and watching them sink to the bottom.

Sliding on the bowling aisles
when you go too far.

Pressing your mum's car horn
and scaring people with it.

Suleman Butt (9)
Ashley Road School

Tell Me If You Like . . .

Tell me if you like . . .
jumping on waves
as they come rolling onto the sand.

Tell me if you like . . .
acting very posh
when relatives come to stay.

Tell me if you like . . .
staring out the window and daydreaming
when you're meant to be doing maths.

Emma Alderson (9)
Ashley Road School

Seasons - Haikus

Beautiful flowers
Green grass staring to grow now
Blossom on the trees

Sun is really hot
Holidays in Italy
Lakes, mountains and trees

Red and yellow leaves
Falling all around the ground
It is windy now

Need to wrap up warm
The snow was here yesterday
Christmas will be soon.

Julia Lamont (9)
Ashley Road School

Tell Me If You Like . . .

Taking a present from under the Christmas tree
and feeling it so that you know whether it's a DVD or a book

. . . watching people stick baked beans up their nose

. . . mashing up ice cream until it's liquid.

Finlay McRobert (9)
Ashley Road School

Tell Me If You Like . . .

Tell me if you like . . .
completing something boring

Tell me if you like . . .
doing something you have never done before

Tell me if you like . . .
feeding birds when they are hungry.

Arun Wardley (9)
Ashley Road School

Ayla's Game

Ayla is my name.
I have a favourite game.
It is called 'Ayla's Game'.
You mix up your friends' names
And guess who they are.
Can you guess who Ayla's friends are?
nasuS nanA ouseiL mulaC mJaes.

Ayla MacDonald-Ludlow (7)
Fetterangus Primary School

Noisy You!

A big snappy crocodile waiting for a treat.
A big cock-a-doodle-doo from a big *noisy* cockerel.
A howl from a wolf and a croak from a frog,
A hiss from a snake,
A jumping kangaroo.
A very quiet mouse
And a very noisy you!

Anna Strachan (7)
Fetterangus Primary School

My Dog

My dog is so funny,
You could say she is mad!
Digs up the garden,
Yes, sometimes she is bad!
Grips onto me when I go to school,
Runs round the room when I get back.
But most of the time,
She makes me feel glad! Glad! Glad!

Calum Ritchie (7)
Fetterangus Primary School

Trudi The Super Dog

My dog is a super dog,
A cute and fluffy dog,
A run-around-the-park dog,
But mostly . . .
A mad, mad, mad dog!

James Smith (7)
Fetterangus Primary School

The Flu

Atishoo! Atishoo! Atishoo!
Oh dear, I have the flu!
My brother said, 'Bless you!'
Cos I was feeling blue!
Atishoo! Atishoo! Atishoo!

Susan Lunan (8)
Fetterangus Primary School

Big Sister

I have a big sister,
She is much bigger than me.
I am so little,
I have to look up to her.
She goes to the academy,
I go to primary.
She is a bit selfish,
I am a bit selfish.
But most of the time,
We get on fine!
I love her,
She loves me,
Sisters forever and ever.

Gemma Stables (9)
Fetterangus Primary School

Fairies

Fairies are my favourite.
They are smaller than me.
They fly around the garden
And live up in a tree.
They sing in the treetops
And dance all day
And with their friends,
They love to play.
Their wings are beautiful and colourful,
But very fragile and breakable.
So be extremely careful if you see,
A tiny fairy playing with me.

Anna O'Farrell (9)
Fetterangus Primary School

James Bond

J aunty
A gile
M ysterious
E nergetic
S ecretive

B rave
O utstanding
N imble
D angerous.

Alex Ewart (8)
Fetterangus Primary School

Darkness

I am scared of darkness.
Darkness, darkness, somewhere *not* to be.
Monsters, monsters, scary to me.
When the power goes out, light the candles real bright.
I am *not* scared of darkness.
Darkness, darkness, somewhere to be.
Monsters, monsters, *not* scary to me.

Jordan Osler (8)
Fetterangus Primary School

Places

P laces, places, somewhere to be.
L ittle or big, but huge to me!
A ustralia is big and Scotland is small.
C ities are big too and villages are not big at all.
E veryone lives in one of these.
S cotland is the best for me, it's the one I choose.

Owen Gillanders (8)
Fetterangus Primary School

Bird - Tanka

All birds have a beak
And they have feathery wings.
Some are colourful
And some are all one colour.
They like to fly in the sky.

Emma Gillanders (10)
Fetterangus Primary School

Maddy

My dog is called Maddy.
My dog is a Lhasa Apso.
My dog is small and fluffy.
My dog is light brown.
My dog has a long tail.
My dog has floppy ears.
My dog has small teeth.
My dog is playful.
My dog likes walks.
My dog hates baths!
My dog watches TV!
My dog has a dog . . .
And she brings it to me.

Ewan Ritchie (9)
Fetterangus Primary School

The Ice Skaters

Ice skaters are nice,
They wear pretty dresses.
They twirl up into the sky
And then they start dancing to the music.
Then they finish with a bow.

Sophie Will (9)
Fetterangus Primary School

Football

Football is fun when you kick the ball.
Football is fun when you score a goal.
Football is fun when you play 'attack'.
Football is fun when you have to run back.

Football is fun when you play with your team.
Football is fun when you win the World Cup.
Football is fun when you meet Martin O'Neil.
Football is fun when you do a back heel.

Daniel Lewczenko (10)
Fetterangus Primary School

When I Grow Up!

When I grow up, what could I do?
I could be a teacher or work in a zoo!
I could be a cleaner, an artist and much, much more.
But I don't want a job that will be a bore!
I could be a drama teacher,
Now that would be fun!
All the children I could teach,
All the things I could preach!
I would enjoy that,
And if I'm lucky -
I'll get a pat on the back!

Chelsea Jade Osler (10)
Fetterangus Primary School

Manchester United

M anchester United,
A re the best team to me.
N ow they are the . . .
C hampions!
H ampden Park is smaller than Old Trafford.
E dwin van der Sar is the goalkeeper.
S ir Alex Ferguson is the manager.
T he other teams must watch out,
E ven the best teams.
R ooney, Ronaldo and Ryan Giggs are my favourite players

U nited they stand,
N ever they fall.
I 've been to Old Trafford,
T he stadium is huge,
E xcellent are the players.
D efenders watch out, United are about!

Marc Andrew Noble (10)
Fetterangus Primary School

Celtic Park Stadium

C eltic is one of the best teams in the world.
E njoyable to watch.
L ennon is the captain.
T hey always seem to impress me.
I watch them on TV.
C eltic Park is where the 'Bhoys' play.

P aul Hartley has just moved to Celtic
A nd Steven Pressley too.
R ight winger is Nakamura.
K enny Miller is my favourite player.

S ome players get a red card.
T homas Gravesen plays centre midfield.
A rtur Boruc is the goalkeeper.
D efenders never give up for Celtic.
I will always support them.
U nder 21s are working hard,
M aybe some day they will play for the first team.

Bruce Lunan (10)
Fetterangus Primary School

Mouse - Haiku

A mouse's tail is
so long and thin, it is a
bit like a small pin.

Laura Buchan (11)
Fetterangus Primary School

Clouds - Haiku

Clouds float by so high,
In the sky they fly right by.
They're so great and soft.

Matthew Cowie (12)
Fetterangus Primary School

Butterflies

Butterflies are beautiful, colourful creatures.
They fly by nibbling nectar.
Their wings are wonderful, butterflies are beautiful.

Laura Whyte (12)
Fetterangus Primary School

Friends

My friends are fun,
They make me laugh.
When I feel sad,
They make me happy.
They share their sweets
And they make me smile.
I would like to keep them for a while!

Louise Anderson (7)
Fetterangus Primary School

Seasons

Bulbs are popping through now
It's that time of year
The Easter bunny is coming
But children do not fear

Light nights here at last
Ice cream and holidays
Oh what a blast
For summer is now here

Walking through the crunchy leaves
As Hallowe'en is near
Passing all the bare trees
In the cold autumn season

Time for snowmen and Christmas cheer
As the last season comes along
People sing and dance away
As they have a Happy New Year.

Holly Coleman (11)
Glashieburn Primary School

Autumn Falls

All the leaves come off the trees
And away go the bumblebees.
Hibernation is all so near
So go to sleep for the winter little bear.
All the leaves are golden red
And all the rabbits have gone to bed.

All the squirrels gather their nuts,
No maybes, no ifs, no buts.
The sun has gone from dusk to dawn,
Winter's on its way.

Grant Andrew Adam Simpson (11)
Glashieburn Primary School

In The Summertime

Summer is such a wonderful time
To spend all day in the warm sunshine
Spending time with friends and having fun
And playing until the sun has gone

Time for barbecues and ice cream
Time for water guns and getting wet
Loads of football and lots of fun
How I love the summertime

All the flowers are in full bloom
Trees are green and are ready to climb
Everything smells so lovely and clean
When it's summertime

But the best thing I love about summertime
Is . . . no more school for a whole six weeks
No more teachers and no more homework
Oh how I love the summertime.

Callum McIntyre (11)
Glashieburn Primary School

The Seasons Poem

In the spring the Welsh flower blooms,
In the summer the marigolds awaken,
In the autumn the gladiolus fill rooms,
In the winter snowdrops are a-shaken.

The newborn arrive in spring,
The new baby birds flying,
The new, now old birds may have a bad wing,
Shh a lot of animals sleep, I'm not lying.

When it's spring, it's warm yet cool,
The summer is a heatwave,
In autumn you may need a cagoule,
In winter heat you will save.

In spring we plant the seeds,
In summer to the seaside we go,
In autumn it's time for weeds,
In winter we play in the snow.

Grant David Smith (11)
Glashieburn Primary School

Autumn

The beautiful colours of the leaves
Red, brown, yellow and green
It may be getting colder
But the fun starts here

The children play
Laughing too
They are having fun
But the fun starts here

The October holidays are coming
You might go on holiday
Or you might not
But the fun starts here.

Andrew John Lowe (11)
Glashieburn Primary School

Summer

We all love summer
So when will it come?
Nobody can wait
To sit outside and get a tan

I wish it would come
So I can play outside
Throwing tennis balls
Instead of snowballs

I want it to come
I really can't wait
I want to do so many things
Apart from making snowmen

It's just around the corner
It just won't come
I want to do things in the sun
I can't wait, oh why won't it come?

Cara Thomson (11)
Glashieburn Primary School

Winter Poem

Sparkly snowflakes falling on the ground
Melting in the stormy rain
Children go out to play
And make some friendly snowmen!

Stepping on the crunchy leaves
Snow covering the bare trees
Icicles hanging from the frozen roof
Dripping onto the icy ground!

All the children are wearing cosy clothes
Jack Frost is coming so wrap up warm or
He'll nip your nose
And bite your ears!

Snow covering the crystal ground
Children's footprints show the fun they've had
The snowflakes dance to the ground
Covering everything in sight!

Kim Cruickshank (11)
Glashieburn Primary School

Winter

Winter is coming
Snow has started falling
Kids are inside
But soon they'll be snowballing

Winter is here
Snow is on the ground
We can now make snowmen
No grass to be found

Winter is leaving
Snow's starting to melt
Nights are fairly stretching
Time for the sledge to be sold

Winter's now gone
Spring's on its way
Flowers are blooming
Oh what a beautiful day.

Macaulay Rae (11)
Glashieburn Primary School

Summer Sun

The summer sun's heat beaming down
Making everybody take off tops and they start to sweat
It is irresistible not to sunbathe
You have to take half a bottle of sun lotion, the heat is so hot

Children playing on the beach
The heat is outstanding, they can't take it
So they end up running down to the sea
A big sigh of relief as they get in the cool refreshing seawater

The flowers grow taller as the sun makes them stronger
Sunflowers grow huge, the gravity can't stop them
Roses are red as the love spreads
Violets are purple and brightly coloured

The sky is clear not a cloud in sight
Just the sun in the sky pushing its blazing heat down
The grass is greener by each summer day
Strawberries forever so sweet, apples shining brightly

The boiling heat begins to die
As autumn withers the sunshine decreases
Colder and colder it gets
Winter breaks through, clouds start to swarm, beating the sunshine.

Scott Wood (11)
Glashieburn Primary School

Winter Poem

Winter is so very cold
So I'm often told
I love the snow and ice
They actually taste very nice!
And the icicles hanging from my nose
Simply match the ice cubes on my toes.

Chloe Mathewson (11)
Glashieburn Primary School

Winter

Snowflakes falling on the ground
All different shapes and sizes
Everything turning white

Hanging silver icicles on the roof
Like small daggers ready to fall
Everything turning white

There is no water for the birds
Only pools of ice, cold and hard
Some birds don't stay but fly south
Where it's warmer

Everything turning white
But soon . . .
Colours will once again appear.

Adam Clark (11)
Glashieburn Primary School

Springtime

Flowers popping up all around
I can hear the birds sing
Lots of colours cover the ground

Days are getting longer
The sun is getting stronger

Trees and bushes were bare
Now buds are pushing way up there

The fly rods are out and start to quiver
As the salmon start to run the river
Lambs and bunnies dance in fields
As spring, its glory, is revealed!

Jordan Strachan (11)
Glashieburn Primary School

I Seem To Be A Cow But I'm Really A Chocolate

They say my name is Daisy,
I hear you asking how,
I'm really fat and lazy,
Because I seem to be a cow!
I like to eat some chocolate,
I know it will make you think,
But then how else would you get a chocolate drink!

Carrie McNeil (11)
Glashieburn Primary School

The Four Seasons

Spring brings all the young; bunnies, lambs and calves,
It's a new year for everyone; let's make it full of laughs!
In the two weeks out of school we celebrate Easter day,
We roll our eggs down a hill and chase them all the way!

Summer's three months are June, July and August,
Just by a fraction, July is the hottest.
Lazing by the beach is the main attraction for some,
While others spend their time having *loads* of fun!

Autumn is the time when the temperature starts to descend
And for most of the trees, their leaves are at their end.
They fall down gracefully, covering the ground,
With a carpet of colour; red, yellow and brown.

Winter comes with Christmas cheer,
But now we are at the end of the year.
A snowman comes and takes over the garden,
Our very own private warden.

Anna Thikey (11)
Glashieburn Primary School

The Season Of . . .

The season of newborn and my birthday too,
The buds on the trees open to the sun,
Animals are born and bulbs poke through,
April, my birthday, oh what fun

The season of sunshine and cloudless skies,
Sandy beaches and ice cream
Long days and long lies,
Oh, how summer is like a dream.

The season of leaves hitting the ground,
Crunchy noises on gold and red paths,
Squirrels search for food all around,
They can't find food in the huge leaf-bath.

The season of festive joy,
Stay up to hear the bells at New Year,
Christmas and New Year bring cards and toys,
Back to spring, for another year!

Grant MacKenzie (11)
Glashieburn Primary School

Summer Madness

In the summer when it's hot,
My grandma turns into a purple robot.
Her favourite food is blueberry ice cream
And to swim in the sea is her lifelong dream.

My grandad's garden is his pride and joy,
He cuts his grass with a huge wind-up toy.
Barbecues and picnics he loves to host,
But because he burns it we settle for toast.

Sandy beach holidays are really so funny,
As when my brother gets wet he turns into a bunny.
Building sandcastles is what he likes to do,
But unfortunately, he likes to eat them too.

As you can see from my family tree,
Summer really is an exciting time for me.
Obviously I'm as perfect as perfect can be,
But . . . when the sun goes down,
Well, you'll just have to wait and see!

Courtney Louise Watt (11)
Glashieburn Primary School

Seasons

Winter is here
And now it's very cold
The snow is falling
Soft, white and fluffy

Now spring has come
And so has the sun
It is very hot
And all the flowers are blooming

Summer has arrived
And there's no school for six weeks
It's time to go on holiday
Hooray! I can't wait

Autumn is here
So it's not so warm
The leaves are falling
Red, orange and brown.

Daniel Smith (11)
Glashieburn Primary School

Winter

Winter is my favourite,
Season of them all.
The only thing I like
Is to watch the snow fall.

It is all so frosty,
All lovely, crisp and cold.
When it all starts to fall,
It is comfortable to hold.

You can have fun with it,
Sprinkle, fight or play.
But as long as it is winter,
Be enthusiastic all day.

Matthew Lee (11)
Glashieburn Primary School

Summer

On the first day of June, I awake and rub my eyes,
To see the sunshine glow through my curtains, vivid and radiant.
Summertime is present; spring has taken its final bow,
Just the opening show, to what my eyes see now.

I look up at the sky, shimmering like the Caribbean Sea,
As clear as a glass of beautifully fresh water,
The sun begins to shine brightly, up in the sky,
Late to bed, early to rise.

The colour from the flowers portray an artful mosaic,
With elegant, swaying green trees as the canvas.
The grass fries like chips in a deep fat fryer,
Birds singing, bees buzzing, wasps stinging make my brother
go higher.

Burgers sizzling on the barbecue,
Perfect weather for a round or two.
School is out, on my way to see my grandparents, it's a must,
All that thinking, now it's the end of August!

Ryan Kellingray (11)
Glashieburn Primary School

My Life

My name is Sophie
I'm from Aberdeen
I go to the one and only Glashieburn Primary!

My favourite colour is pink
My favourite film is 'Grease'
My favourite hobbies are dancing and gymnastics
But the one thing I hate is peace

I have a bit of a sweet tooth
I love to sunbathe
I always play with my friends
We always love to run

I like to eat fine food
Especially lots of chocolate
I audition for lots of dances
I am happy when I get through

Well that's about me
Oh I forget one thing
I love to giggle *he he he.*

Sophie Morrice (11)
Glashieburn Primary School

My Wonderful World!

I stepped out of the perfectly purple door
And gazed in amazement.
This wonderful world in front of my eyes was beautiful.

White horses ran with their beautiful hair dancing in the wind,
The grass they ran on was taller than me
And a little home for minibeast.

Brown and white rabbits hopped across
Little black pebbles beside the river.
Trickling water and horses' hooves
Were the only sounds to be heard.

Blue skies with bunny-shaped clouds
Drifted above this wonderful world.
Sometimes covering the marvellous sun,
Causing the animals to run.

All of a sudden I woke up,
My wonderful world has gone.
Maybe tomorrow or maybe not,
I will dream back to

My wonderful world.

Rebecca Louise Gardiner (11)
Glashieburn Primary School

Go Disney!

Fairy dust and fiery pirates,
Casting spells and playing tricks.
With cute little twinkly outfits,
How can you not love the gorgeous Tinkerbell!

With his plump yellow belly
And all his loveable friends,
He nicks the yummy honey from all those angry bees!
Yep you guessed it . . . it's Winnie the Pooh!

With her red, short frocks
And her cheeky chops!
She giggles at funny Mickey,
For this is loveable Minnie!

He lies all day and his nose gets longer,
He just can't stop, he's such a talented liar.
With his old-fashioned waistcoats and shrunken wooden head!
No he's not a real boy . . .
It's the lying foolish Pinocchio!

Emily Jane Reid (10)
Glashieburn Primary School

Seasons

April showers
Welcome new flowers
Warmer weather
It's feeling better

Blue skies
Shining sun
Long, long evenings
Holiday's begun

Autumn leaves
Fall from the trees
Under my feet in the lane
It's getting cold again

Winter is my favourite season
Would you like to know the reason?
It's my birthday and Christmas too
Lots of snow and things to do.

Jae Chang Jang (11)
Glashieburn Primary School

Autumn

As autumn comes
Leaves shall fall
Red, orange and gold
Winter round the bend
Crunch goes the leaves
As people stand on them
Animals think about hibernation
Autumn is colourful
Awash of colours
Like a painting
Leaves like an old treasure map
All crunched up
And beginning to fade
It is a mixed season
Warm with colour, then bare and cold
Winter approaches.

Austin Brown (11)
Glashieburn Primary School

My Year

I like spring 'cause it's no longer dark,
Me and my friends can go back to the park.
It's Easter time; it's my birthday too,
Chocolate eggs and presents new.

Now it's summer there will be no school,
Go on holiday and jump in the pool.
Go out with my friends, play football till late,
When my mum calls me in, I make her wait.

The days are getting colder,
As the year is getting older.
I watch the Catherine wheel turn,
Then I'll watch Guy Fawkes burn.

Will there be presents under the tree?
I wonder what will be waiting for me.
Watch TV, listen to Big Ben,
Another year over, let's do it again!

Daniel Thom (11)
Glashieburn Primary School

Four Seasons

Winter is here,
It's time to cheer.
Lots of snow,
There is plenty to throw.

Summer is a time for fun,
Playing games in the sun.
Ice cream, swimming, sand and sea,
Are the best bits of holidays for me.

Flowers grow in spring
And the birds also sing.
Baby animals everywhere,
A spring feeling in the air.

Autumn brings a rush of leaves,
Falling silently from the trees.
Animals curl up in their nests
To sleep away their winter rest.

Emma Paterson (11)
Glashieburn Primary School

Buddy's Poem

He cheers me up when I am blue
He likes to chew on my mum's shoe
He gets all dirty and muddy outside
As only a dog would do!

He lies and sleeps in the night
Right beside the candlelight
Dreaming of chewing the biggest bone
It'd probably make his stomach hurl

When I take him for a walk in the park
He runs, yaps, growls and barks
He rolls in the grass and licks my hand
Waiting for a biscuit, it's part of his plan

In the morning he licks my ear
As if to say, 'Good morning dear!'
I love my dog, he's so sweet
He looks so cute, he's my best friend.

Beth Alexander (10)
Glashieburn Primary School

Pink Elephants

Why can't elephants be pink?
Who wouldn't want a pink elephant?
With red spots and blue polka dots
That would be the best
Better than seeing a bird's nest

I want a pink elephant
In a blue ballet outfit
Doing a pretty dance
And a little prance

I want a pink elephant
With a heart-shaped trunk
And a friend who is an orange skunk
My pink elephant is the best
Better than all the rest!

Hannah Pirie (10)
Glashieburn Primary School

Winter Poem

The snow was falling down
Boys and girls went sledging
The aliens came and were freezing
Christmas was quick at Grandma's house
The ice was great for skating on
Everyone was laughing

Christmas carollers sang at doors
The turkey came in still wide awake
Watching the children say a grace
Snow looked deep outside the window
As we waited for a snowball fight

People dressed from head to toe
To keep warm in the coldness
Nights fell dark early
But when morning came
The snow was still there.

Jill Orr (11)
Glashieburn Primary School

Cars

There are many in the world,
Exotic, SUVs, hatchbacks and sports cars,
My favourite of all is actually Tuner cars,
Hummers are nice,
Protons are rubbish,
If you need a ride that's blinged out get a Cadillac Escalade,
You want an exotic get a Lamborghini Murcielago,
If you want a hatchback get an Alfa Romeo Brera,
Go to GAS in America to get your ride pimped,
SUVs, cool Hummers, Cadillacs, Range Rovers and many more,
You want a racing car that you can buy, get an Aston Martin DBS9,
So that's my car directory in a poem,
I've got one more thing to mention; my favourite super cars,
Bugatti Veyron, Ferrari Enzo, Aston Martin DBS.
Thanks for reading!

Jamie Melvin (11)
Glashieburn Primary School

Liverpool

The Reds always win
Rafael is ace at buyin' folk in
Stevie G is our ace
Stevie G has heaps of pace

Peter Crouch; lanky boy
He is always full of joy
Luis Garcia is a skilful lad
Even though he can be a bit bad

Harry Kewell puts in an ace cross
But he never gets a game from the boss
Riise is solid at the back
He's probably got a six pack

Craig's amazing foot
Saved him from getting the boot
Durk Kuyt is a goal-scorer
Certainly not a crowd borer

Barcelona one, Liverpool two
Agger goes away with his girl Sue
The rest of the team go away to get a rest
But they keep getting phone calls from the press.

Liverpool, Liverpool are the best!

Adam Corbett (11)
Glashieburn Primary School

Football

Kick the ball in the net,
With your foot or your head,
Score goals and win the game,
It is always just the same.

Ronaldinho skins them all,
Even with a fancy ball.

Shevchenko beats the defence,
Even if they are at their best.

John Terry stops them all,
Especially when he is in a wall.

Nakamura scores free kicks,
Brilliant against Man United!

Chelsea are the best!
Better than the rest!

Blair Milne (10)
Glashieburn Primary School

Liverpool

The Reds go marching in
Always getting a win
Stevie G smacks in goals
And bends free kicks inside the poles
Xabi puts in a super ball
Too bad some players are very small
Peter Crouch has got great height
It gives the players a mighty fright

Liverpool 2, Barcelona 1

They left Barcelona scared and shocked
Liverpool were happy because of the time on the clock
Liverpool are happy for the second leg
Stevie G tries a nutmeg

Liverpool FC

Champions of Europe in 2005
AC Milan said Gerrard dived
Stevie G said it was a lie
As the Liverpool team is in Europe again
The crowd makes as much noise as the clock Big Ben

Now the players are off to bed
With the football match still buzzing in their head

They will be champions of Europe once again.

Liam Tough (11)
Glashieburn Primary School

Liverpool FC

The Liverpool men marching on the pitch,
Mark Gonzalez started to itch.
Durk Kuyt wins a free kick,
Steven Gerrard smacks it in the goal,
It leaves the goalkeeper scratching his moles.

Xabi Alonso is crossing in the ball,
Crouch gets the header, he's very tall.
John Arne Riise goes sliding in hard,
He ends up getting a yellow card.
The match is almost over, it's soon time for bed.

Just at the end Bellamy's hit on the head,
All the players give a big cheer,
All the fans go away for their beer.
They all can't wait for the second leg,
The players can't get over Kuyt's nutmeg.

As they get home they have lots of stress,
It's all because of the stupid press.
The press get into trouble,
Then all the players go and rest.

Mark Elder (10)
Glashieburn Primary School

Football

F unniest sport ever
O h boy I love it
O h yes Man U are the best
T he best player is Cristiano Ronaldo
B awl as loud as you can
A s everyone does so you won't be different
L augh as much as you can when John Terry misses the ball, as
L ong as there is any left, you can always get refreshments
at the stall.

Stuart Duncan (11)
Glashieburn Primary School

Not True!

Elephants wear little skirts and cute tops.
Dogs like to party and dance all night long.
I have a pet made out of jelly.
There is a day in the week called 'Monkey Madness'.

I'm a rabbit, dog, monkey, cat, penguin, panda all in one.
Cats wear hats.
Cows wear donkeys.
Mice weight-lift.

Monkeys ride shoes.
Elephants are pink and blue and are in my shoe.
My blue maths jotter is orange.
Yesterday I went to the cinema and took a front seat at the back.

I'm a shoe and I like going outside.
Elephants are small and my pencil is tall.
Cats talk all night long.
Rabbits like to sing all night long.

Cats always watch 'The Simpsons' on TV.
Penguins sunbathe.
Pandas like to dress up.

Alanna Morrison (10)
Glashieburn Primary School

Hair

Hair is long
Hair is short
If it's not soft
You won't go to court

Calm or puffy
I always brush it
It's always the same
Never tame

Different hairstyles
Can be silly
If mine's too short
It would kill me

Long, short
Spiky, frizzy
Curly, straight
Or ordinary

My hair is
Thick, blonde
Straight and long

And that is how I like it!

Alison De Neui (10)
Glashieburn Primary School

Pink Elephant

I saw a pink elephant
walking on the beach
with a glittering saddle
you could see for a mile

I wanted to ride on its back
but couldn't reach up high
so I went on a giraffe
and sat on its back

I was now on the elephant
right on its back
I couldn't believe it
I was so high up

It walked right forward
along the seashore
it started to run
and splash around

It was a miracle
I just knew it was
then I got a shock
and fell on my back

I was now off the pink elephant
with lovely pink eyes
I loved my ride
but not the fall

I loved the lovely pink elephant ride
so now I will say goodbye!

Jade Collinson (11)
Glashieburn Primary School

Pimped

Cars, cars and more cars
I'll make it jump!
Or I'll make it smart!
SUVs, luxury or exotic, I'll do it
Wanna big one?
Call me!
I'll be in LA or Aberdeen
I'll hook you up
Pinstripe, flames or flags
Lambo, Chevy, Hummer and choppers
I'll bling your car till it shines!
It will stand out in a cool way
If you like bikes I got 'em too
Cars, big cars, bigger cars
I'll pimp your ride!
Pimpin' is what I do!

Calum Mair (11)
Glashieburn Primary School

The Evil Socks

Sometimes I make my own creations, like evil socks
They can be stripy, plain or have chickenpox
Have you ever met a wise pair of shoes?
Like ice skates or even old smelly boots
It doesn't even matter if the laces are tied in knots

My best friends think the evil socks are strange
So I stopped drawing for days and days
I finally moved on and forgot about it
I started to not mind, not one bit
But I still made them secretly out of clay

I stored them just under my bed
Every day, peeking at them, banging my head
I then had to have my room painted pink
So I hid my sculptures behind the sink
'Your room's so dusty!' my mother said

I then spent all day dusting the house
I found loads of things, including my toy mouse
My mum then painted the walls bright pink
I didn't like it, it looked like horrible pink ink
I secretly painted my room the colour of my blue blouse

My mum went mad, more than mad
I didn't care, I was not sad
I started drawing lots of different things
Or making puppets with loads of strings
My room looked like a cave, so I was very glad

I started reading all sorts of books
And buying more fashionable boots
I tried out swimming, ice skating and netball
I went to practise in the gym hall
When I was older, I learned to be an excellent cook.

Katie Ann Thomson (10)
Glashieburn Primary School

Dracula And The Fruit Bowl

Last night I had a sleepover
And Dracula came in a Rover,
He'd painted it purple and blue,
The music was very loud too.

Dracula was getting very hungry
So I said you can have my friend's bunny,
But Dracula refused, he wanted some fruit,
Instead, I gave him some milk and a foot.

He screeched as loud as he could,
I was going to run away, I thought that I could.
Dracula ran down the stairs,
He went to the fruit bowl and grabbed some pears.

My friends ran out of the door,
Now they don't play with me anymore,
Ever since that night that Dracula gave
Me a horrible fright!

Megan Golightly (11)
Glashieburn Primary School

Do I Have A Brain?

No, no, no
I try to think but nothing comes out,
My brain is mushed peas,
I can't even shout,

Why, why, why?
Some people think I'm so smart,
I really am as dumb as a fart,

Do I or do I not?
I can't decide if I have a brain,
I am in a knot,
'Cause I've been caught,

Oh, oh, oh,
What's one add one,
I am so dumb,
No one is my chum,

But if I can write this,
I guess I miss the point of a brain,
Yes! I'm done,
This poem is lame.

Gemma Laura Morgan (10)
Glashieburn Primary School

Cars Go Zooming Down The Street

Cars go zooming down the street
An old lady and its bumpers meet
Nitros comes out of the back
If it's speed that the cars lack
The F1 car is so fast
The other cars are out of sight at last
McLaren is so smart
It is in the lead from the start
The Hummer is really big
It's bigger than an oil rig
Richard Hammond is a driver
He is a car crash survivor
The Koenigsegg is faster
It is the car master!

Jamie Findlay (10)
Glashieburn Primary School

My Brain

I'm flipping over 100-feet-high buildings,
Green and white polka dot flowers.
I am really in Heaven,
I really have magical powers,
I have a lot of fun.

Sunny, cloudy, snowy or rain,
It's too much fun to care,
When I'm dancing in my magical brain,
In the lovely pollution-free air,
This awesome world is *never boring,*
This place is totally the best,
In this place there is no snoring,
So at least you can get some rest.

Here, the fun will never end
Because I'm never alone,
I'm with my totally awesome, carefree imaginary friend!

Lauren Birnie (10)
Glashieburn Primary School

The Night I Dreamt Of Heaven

While I was sleeping
I once thought I was in Heaven
Occasionally I see my grandma
Who died just a year ago

Once I saw an angel
She was beautiful and white
When she went away
I knew she was still watching over me

Once I saw a feather
It was long, fluffy and white
Someone was holding it
But I couldn't quite see who it was

I thought it looked gorgeous
All the way up there in Heaven
But I know it was just a dream.

Christy Birnie (11)
Glashieburn Primary School

The Simpsons

T hey're
H ere at 6pm on Channel 4,
E ver missed it? You can't like it that much.

S illy they may be, but I don't care,
I 'm addicted to them,
M arge, Maggie, Lisa, Homer and Bart are the characters.
P roud as punch I am to watch them,
S ideshow Bob is a maniac,
O ver the TV, Mum shouts, 'Tea is ready.'
N ever miss them!
S tops at 6.30pm.

Lewis Denholm (11)
Glashieburn Primary School

Cats That Are Purple

C ats
A re
T ame
S ometimes I

T hink
H ow
A crobatic
T he cats can be

A nd how they
R un and pounce like when they see their
E nemy

P ouncing
U nder
R oses
P unching the air
L ike
E verything is bad.

Georgia Gifford (10)
Glashieburn Primary School

My Family . . .

My family is really weird,
My grampa Nicol's got a spiky beard!

They just don't know when to stop,
When they are giggling over the top!

We love it when it's May Day,
Then we get to go out to play!

We all love to play the Wii,
Then rest under a shady tree!

My granny's hair is bright green,
As green as a green bean!

We then go to bed at night
And cuddles in the covers so tight!

Paige Wright (11)
Glashieburn Primary School

Thinking Of Family

Watching all the kids go by,
Wishing I had said goodbye,
To all my friends and family,
Full of shame, full of pity.

Getting on the large red train,
By myself and full of pain,
I wish I had someone to talk to,
All alone I wish to get a good carer,
A nice new family.

Sitting in a great big carriage,
Waiting for the train to go,
Sitting lonely, full of regret,
For not saying a proper goodbye.

Missing Mum, missing Dad,
Feeling lonely, feeling sad,
Wishing for all this shame to go,
Wishing I had a sibling to talk to,
Someone to play with,
Someone to help me throughout this journey.

Samuel Hardisty (12)
Kingswells Primary School

Winter Poem

Snow is falling
On the icy ground
Making it all white
As it stays still.

The birds fly
Past the glittery white trees
Singing merrily
With joyful Christmas songs.

Children building snowmen
Having lots of fun
Dressing it up
As the snow falls softly.

The children wrap up warmly
Wearing their hats and scarves
Having fun sleighing down the hills
And throwing snowballs.

Natalia McQueen (11)
Glashieburn Primary School

Away, Away

Away, away on a train,
Away, away, away from pain,
I'm going away from the city,
Away, away from those who I pity,
But I know I'll return again.

The country, the country, oh how nice,
The country, the country, home of mice,
I feel under the weather,
As light as a feather,
When I go home will it be better?

Ryan Mennie (11)
Kingswells Primary School

Evacuation

Goodbye my mother,
I'll see you again,
When the war is over,
When the bombs are gone.

We got on the train,
Me and my sister,
It was small and cramped,
Like our classroom at school.

We waved Mother goodbye
And started to cry and weep,
As the train left the station,
We sat down, tears running down our faces.

It was a bumpy journey,
There was no toilet or food,
We rushed past flowers and villages,
All a blur of colour and light.

We wanted to go home,
But we knew we couldn't,
We were safe in the country,
Away from the bombers.

We arrived in the town,
The little town of Echt,
It was very beautiful,
But would we like it here?

Callum McCaw (11)
Kingswells Primary School

Away From Home

I hate being away from home,
Far away from home.

I shouldn't be here,
Why am I here?
Far away from home.

I love my family,
I love my friends,
But they want me to be safe,
Far away from home.

As tears roll down my face,
As I think of my mum,
I know why she did this
And that's why I'm far away from home.

Bryony Manson (12)
Kingswells Primary School

The Train Journey

I'm all alone,
The people around me are quiet,
I feel unhappy,
My mum and dad would be eating now,
So far, I have been on the train for 4 hours,
I am starving,
My brother and sister are gone.

In the background, I can hear the train,
It was going clickety-clack,
My head, full of worry about what is in store for me,
I am missing my family and friends,
No one in my cabin is talking.

I'm all alone,
I wish that I had eaten more before I left home,
All I took was my teddy bear and doll,
I wish that the war was over and I could go home,
I just really want to go home.

Christy Young (11)
Kingswells Primary School

Goodbye, Goodbye

My stomach rumbled in nerves,
I ate my breakfast with my mum,
Nearly in tears,
'Goodbye, goodbye, see you when I get back.'

Getting on the train was a nightmare,
Hundreds of children,
I grabbed my sister's hand
And jumped on,
Waving to my mum goodbye.

The boy in the carriage smelt a bit bad,
There was tears, fear, excitement and chatting,
I soothed my sister when she cried,
The train was as noisy as an old loud Hoover.

The green hills were beautiful,
The pink powerful make-up from my sister was horrible,
We passed the dark forest
And the nice flowers as well,
What will happen next?
I asked myself.

Ross Yule (11)
Kingswells Primary School

No Place Like Home

I feel sad,
I feel so sad,
I feel excited too,
I can't wait till the day I come home,
The day I come home to you.

My stomach is grumbling,
My belly is aching,
The food in my bag is all gone,
How I wish I had some more food in my bag,
A little more food, just some.

The smells are awful,
The smells are so awful,
The boy next to me was sick,
The carriage I'm in smells horrific,
I wish I were home with you.

I see lots of houses,
Some lovely houses,
I see lots of animals too,
Oh how I wish,
I wish I were home with you.

Stuart Close (11)
Kingswells Primary School

On The Train

Clitter-clatter, clitter-clatter, on the track,
Nothing but a gas mask in my sack,
I miss my family, I miss my home,
I want to turn this train around and go back.

Clitter-clatter, clitter-clatter, train moves on,
I've got nobody, I'm all alone,
I hate this journey, I hate this war,
I'm too sad to even moan.

Clitter-clatter, clitter-clatter,
Fields pass by,
Full of cattle as I start to cry,
When will this devastating war end?
And why was I evacuated, why oh why?

Clitter-clatter, clitter-clatter,
Train stands still,
Inside my body I start to feel ill,
I look outside the iron beast
And see the station start to fill.

Clitter-clatter, clitter-clatter, my heart goes,
Who will take me from the country?
No one knows,
Tears begin to roll down my face
And now my head is full of woes.

Clitter-clatter, clitter-clatter,
When the bombs are gone,
I'll see my family when the war is won,
So why do I miss my family so much?
I just can't wait until the war is done.

Alex Christides (11)
Kingswells Primary School

I Wish

The children's shouts are piercing,
They're loud and inconsiderate,
I wish I were with my family,
I dream of being with my parents again.

I smell the manure from outside the train,
I smell the children from inside the train,
I wish I were with my family,
I dream of being with my parents again.

My younger brother grabs my hand tightly,
As I wrap my arm around him - shaking,
I wish I were with my family,
I dream of being with my parents again.

Strange-looking animals wander around fields,
Carelessly eating patches of grass, ignoring the train,
I wish I were with my family,
I dream of being with my parents again.

As the vehicle comes to a halt,
I see scary faces smiling from the ground,
I wish I were with my family,
I dream of being beside them, now . . .

Taylor Gardner (11)
Kingswells Primary School

Waiting

Waiting with my mum,
Waiting for the train,
Waiting for my biscuits to call out my name,
Walking up the hallway,
Walking past the children,
Walking up to my seat,
Crying for my mum,
Crying for my dad,
Crying for my family,
I wish I were still at home,
I wish I were still with my mum,
I wish wishes could really come true!

Amy Sinclair (11)
Kingswells Primary School

Going To The Country

I'm on the train, going to Banff,
I'm scared and cold, I need my mum,
I can see walking clouds, but my older sister calls them sheep,
I miss my dad, he's in the RAF.

The train's chugging along the track,
I want to go home, take me back.

I want to see where I will go, will I be poor
Or shall I be rich? I feel so hungry,
Tired and bored, I need my mum now,
I'm really scared.

Stuart Banks (11)
Kingswells Primary School

Far Away

I'm on the train, on the train,
Going far away, far away,
Away from Mum, from Mum,
Away from Dad, from Dad,
Away from home, from home,
Far, far away, far away.

I feel sad when I think about my family,
I feel excited when I think about the country,
I feel worried when I think about getting split up
From my brothers,
I feel happy when I think about meeting the farm animals.

I'm on my way, on my way,
I'm on my way, far away.

Natasha Hassard (12)
Kingswells Primary School

The Countryside

In the countryside,
It was a very peaceful day,
But yet it was very hard,
To wipe our feelings away.

The birds were tweeting calmly,
As calm as the wind,
But yet it was very hard,
To find a normal friend.

I've longed to go home,
This is my last glimpse of the countryside sun,
But yet it is very hard,
Now that the time to go home has come.

Richard Dobeson (11)
Kingswells Primary School

Can I Come Home To You?

Mother, why are you doing this to me?
Don't send me away to this family,
Where am I going?
Will I ever see you again?
I can see clouds with legs,
I can see big fat dogs,
I can't ask you what they are
Because you are at home.

I really don't want to go,
Can't I stay home with you?
What should I do if I don't
Like the family?

I've put you away to keep you safe,
Of course you will see me again,
I'll tell you all about the animals,
When you come home again,
No you can't stay home with me
Because you might get hurt,
If you don't like the family,
Just think about me.

Mitchell Derek Scott (11)
Kingswells Primary School

Evacuation

I'm on the train, going away,
I'll be there soon on the farm,
I want to go home, to see my mum,
The lady I'm with is really mean.

My dad might die in the war,
I want to go home, I'm scared and cold,
I need my mum right now.

Scott Mitchell (11)
Kingswells Primary School

On The Train

Babies don't stop crying,
The smelly bins on the train stink,
Funny animals that look like clouds stand in the fields,
The thought of my dad in the war is frightening,
So is the thought of my mum on her own.

The rain lashing off the window is horrible,
The sound of the train makes me feel annoyed,
I could picture five years in a country house,
Playing cricket and ball.

Mark Alexander Birnie (11)
Kingswells Primary School

Leaving

I'm sick of the train,
I'm sick of the pain,
Nothing outside but the pouring rain,
I'm all alone, too sad to moan,
Chit-chat, the people talk and drone.

I miss my mum,
I miss my dad,
I have nothing but a notepad,
My brother is fighting,
I hope he's writing home.

I'm sick of the war,
It's gone too far,
Make it stop or else I'll pop.

Callum Shinnie (11)
Kingswells Primary School

The Evacuee Train

Some nights I cannot sleep,
Because tomorrow I might weep.

I feel sad, I don't know why,
Because normally I never cry.

The next day I arose,
But when I saw the train, I almost froze.

It was so horrid,
Hardly homely.

Bang and crash the train went,
I wish I were home,
I sat there and dreamt.

Sophie Perrott (11)
Kingswells Primary School

Whole Story

Goodbye Mum,
Goodbye Dad,
Goodbye my brothers and sisters,
Farewell, farewell as I go off in this train,
I love you, I love you and I will never forget you,
On a train, a big bad train,
That will take me away from you,
Wearily there to the place that's new to me,
Don't like it here, don't like it here,
It's as cramped as a small compartment.

Coming home, coming home,
The war has ended now,
Can't wait till I come home to you,
To a little town called Louth.

Shaun Lane (11)
Kingswells Primary School

On The Train

It was raining outside of the train,
There were bad smells on the train,
There were no toilets on the train,
People crying on the train.

People crying like newborn babies,
People snuffling like they had a cold,
Raindrops are bullets outside of the train.

The smells were horrible and horrid,
Feeling upset on the train,
Feeling excited on the train,
Missing Mum and Dad,
Wondering when I'll get home,
Wondering if the war will mend,
I just wanted this all to end!

Callum Kemp (11)
Kingswells Primary School

When I Went Away

I kiss goodbye
And start to cry,
As I get on the train,
I feel the pain.

The boy sitting next to me is mad
And his smell is also bad,
My stomach starts to rumble,
As I shiver and mumble.

I miss my mum so,
As I start to go,
The tears drip down
And I start to frown.

We arrive at the station
And I think of the frustration,
I want to run,
Because I just can't have any fun.

Bethany Buchanan (11)
Kingswells Primary School

The Train Journey

I've not eaten in an hour,
I'm packing up, don't forget teddy,
Goodbye everyone, Mum I'm ready.

I didn't know it would take so long,
I guess my calculations were wrong,
Getting taken in, my people are fussy,
The bombs are falling while I'm in bed.

The war's been going on for 3 weeks, so I read,
I'm so upset, I can't stop crying,
I can't sleep, it feels like I'm dying.

'I want to go home,'
I say as I roam,
This feels like a new life,
I want to go home desperately.

Georgia Harkins (11)
Kingswells Primary School

Want To Go Home

Want to go home,
Want to go home,
Want to go home,
Just want to go home.

Feel so sad,
Miss the family,
Hope Dad kills the enemies,
Just want to go home.

Boy beside me smells so bad,
The condensed milk made me shiver,
This did not smell nice,
Just want to go home.

Stuck my head out the window to see the sights,
Girl in front was sick, that did not look nice,
Everybody looks different,
Just want to go home.

Most people were talking,
Rustling with wrappers,
Crying with fear,
Just want to go home.

Cuddled with teddy,
Tears dribbled off my face,
Hoped war would be over soon,
Just want to go home.

Megan Maver (11)
Kingswells Primary School

All Gone

No more bombs in sight, all gone,
No more dogfights in sight, all gone,
No more swastikas in sight, all gone,
No more air raids to fight, all gone,
No more Germans marching in town, all gone.

I am free at last, free like the wind,
I need my family now, all I need are my friends,
I need to leave but I'm in England,
How can I get to Germany?

I am all gone.

Jordan McQueen (12)
Kingswells Primary School

The Journey Away From Home

I take my pillow on the train,
Feeling very sad.

I have my toy,
But I am still not feeling very glad.

Instead I am feeling bad about leaving
My home.

Kyle Baker (11)
Kingswells Primary School

On The Tracks

Sitting alone on the train,
Watching tiny drops of rain,
I wave goodbye to Mum and Dad,
Thinking of the good times we've had,
Listening to the children whine and moan,
I shall be going to a place unknown.

Glen Cairns (12)
Kingswells Primary School

Going Away

I come out of my house and walk down the road,
I head for the station, past all of the houses and shops,
I am glad to be away from all of the bombs,
As I sit on the train, ready to go,
All of the children are talking and crying,
I sit in the corner waiting to leave,
I can't wait to see my new family
And all of the things in the country.

Niall MacDonald (11)
Kingswells Primary School

The Countryside

I smell a lot of fresh air,
The country is so nice,
I see a lot of animals,
Like sheep, cows and mice.

There is a lot of trees,
Some are fat and some are small,
Some are skinny
And some are tall.

Lots of birds are singing,
Very lovely songs,
I enjoy listening to them,
As I travel along.

My journey is almost over,
The country is so nice,
I enjoyed my journey,
Did you enjoy it too?

Samantha Mitchell (11)
Kingswells Primary School

War Poem

My name is Henry,
Henry is my name,
I'm heading out of London,
I'm going on a train.

I'm an evacuee,
An evacuee I am,
I'm going to the country,
The first time I'll see a ram.

I am very sad,
Very sad I am,
I'm leaving Mum and Dad,
I'm leaving my cat, Tam.

Although I really miss them,
I really miss them I do,
The country isn't too bad,
Apart from the cow poo.

If only I could go home,
If only I could leave,
But this war will never stop,
We'll just have to believe.

Robbie Collinson (11)
Kingswells Primary School

Keep Me Here Or Put Me Away

Where will I go?
As far as the North Pole?
Please *No!*
I'm *not* going.

Keep me here,
Don't put me on the smelly train.

The train might smell of sick,
What if I go far away?

I have to go away from you,
Please *No!*

Lucie Walker Chalmers (11)
Kingswells Primary School

The Train And My Life

Train on the track,
It won't turn back,
Train on the track,
It won't turn back,
Train on the track,
I beg you to turn back.

My life should be happy but it's sad,
I feel furious, miserable, denied, mad,
My life in the city was so much fun,
Now I hate my new life that has unfortunately begun,
My life is ruined, my life is done,
Goodbye happiness, goodbye fun.

Ricky Elrick (11)
Kingswells Primary School

Happiness

Happiness is red like strawberry yoghurt,
It sounds like someone laughing,
It tastes like white chocolate,
It smells like ice cream,
Happiness looks like vanilla ice cream,
It feels like putting suncream on,
It reminds me of going to the beach.

Emma Barry (7)
Methlick Primary School

Happiness

Happiness is white like a woolly sheep,
It sounds like bumping downstairs,
It tastes like Polo mints,
It smells like the air outside,
Happiness looks like a big duvet,
It feels like fluffy feathers,
It reminds me of a sleepover at Jade's.

Rebecca Gammack (8)
Methlick Primary School

Fear Factory

Fear is black like the darkest night,
It sounds like glass smashing,
It tastes like a mouldy melon,
It smells like Lauren's rotten socks,
Fear looks like a cold skeleton,
It feels like a spider crawling up your arm,
It reminds me of a bad dream.

Bayley Jarvis (7)
Methlick Primary School

The Laughter Outside

Laughter is golden like the shining sun,
It sounds like bells and a stream in the middle of the trees,
It tastes like a sweet, sweet golden melon,
It smells like the air outside,
Laughter looks like birds singing happily at the beach,
It feels like touching something tickly,
It reminds me of laughing in your dreams.

Martha Macmillan (7)
Methlick Primary School

Laughter

Laughter is yellow like the sun shining,
It sounds like tapping the table,
It tastes like spaghetti,
It smells like Polo mints,
Laughter looks like ice cream,
It feels like goodness,
It reminds me of good days.

Rebecca Thompson (7)
Methlick Primary School

Darkness

Darkness is black like a freezing night,
It sounds like the wind blowing through my hair,
It tastes like bitter lemon,
It smells like fresh seawater,
Darkness looks like Dracula,
It feels like cold solid concrete,
It reminds me of seeing shadows at the school.

Jade Aikenhead (8)
Methlick Primary School

Sadness And Tears

Sadness is white like a cow,
It sounds like rain on a shed,
It tastes like soggy cabbages,
It smells like rotten carrots,
Sadness looks like dropping rain,
It feels like black blood,
It reminds me of smelly rats.

Andrew Connon (8)
Methlick Primary School

Love

Love is red like strawberry jam,
It sounds like Christmas bells,
It tastes like romance and kissing in the sun,
It smells like strawberry cream,
Love looks like roses,
It feels like a cuddly bear,
It reminds me of my birthday last year.

Louise Gammack (8)
Methlick Primary School

Hugs And Kisses

Love is red like hearts,
It sounds like baby kisses,
It tastes like my mum's chocolate cake,
It smells like lovely roses,
Love looks like gentle hugs,
It feels like very, very soft silk,
It reminds me of all of us in Mum and Dad's bed!

Kirsten Glen (8)
Methlick Primary School

Poké Poem

Darkness is like Gengar,
It sounds like Rayquaza rushing through the air,
It tastes like Gastly's gas,
It smells like Grimer,
Darkness looks like Pikachu using Thunder,
It feels like Groudon's spikes,
It reminds me of all sorts of Pokémon.

Jonathan Howitt (8)
Methlick Primary School

Anger

Anger is black like Mewtwo,
It sounds like Moltres flying through the air,
It tastes like Gastly's gas,
It smells like Grimer sliding through the ruins,
Anger looks like Swampert in a swamp,
It feels like Groudon's spikes,
It reminds me of dark Pokémon.

Harry McNutt (8)
Methlick Primary School

The Sky

The sky is blue,
Like a cockatoo.
But another day,
It could be grey.
When the sky's fine,
It really is divine.
It's home to the bird of peace,
The dove's feathers don't have a single crease.
Some say the sky's mood,
Can change the weather from bad to good.
Others reckon God decides,
Whether or not the rain is like pesticide.
Is the sky the sign of freedom or not?
This may be the question that will make our brains rot.
On the other hand, what is the sky's true colour?
This is also a real brain-puzzler.

Liam Boston (12)
Middleton Park Primary School

Homework

Homework, homework, I hate homework,
Especially on a Saturday night,
You do it every day, you do it every night,
I hate homework on a Saturday night
Maths, language, science or art, you do it every day,
It's a pain!

Rachel Dawson (11)
Middleton Park Primary School

Ryan

There once was a boy called Ryan,
Who was awfully scared of flying,
He went into the plane,
It took off in the rain,
Now he can't stop sobbing and crying.

Ryan Dunn (12)
Middleton Park Primary School

Evil Frosty The Snowman!

F lying in his dream,
R eading naughty books,
O n a Sunday morning,
S inging on the clouds,
T elling his evil memories,
Y elling at his ambassadors.

T ell your friends,
H e's not as good as Superman,
E at you, he will.

S o now he's licking his lips,
N ow he sights his enemies,
O n their way to him,
W anting them eagerly,
M ore than Santa,
A s they arrive,
N ow he's very happy.

Connor James Robb (11)
Middleton Park Primary School

Feelings

We can sometimes feel glad
And sometimes feel sad,
We're sometimes cheerful
And sometimes feel tearful.

We're sometimes feeling helpful,
For doing things right,
We're sometimes feeling pitiful,
For hiding out of sight.

Feelings are full of power,
Every minute on the hour,
We can even be fearful,
Joyful and grateful.

I sometimes feel strong,
Like I'm 10 foot tall,
But I sometimes feel weak,
As if I'm 3 foot small.

When all of your feelings,
Are mixed in together,
You get something new,
Which will last forever.

Nadia Imbabi (11)
Middleton Park Primary School

Birthdays

Birthdays are great,
You can stay up late,
Put up balloons,
While listening to your favourite tunes,
Have a great big chocolate cake
And stay up late,
While having a sleepover with your mate.

Your mum puts out delicious food
And eat it you should!
Now it's time to open your gifts,
All your new clothes are perfect fits.

Party games are great too,
Because all you have to do,
Is get the music playing,
Here comes the postman with a card saying,
'Happy birthday, enjoy your day.'

Here comes the cake, it's time to say Happy Birthday,
Have a brilliant day!

Ellen Shand (11)
Middleton Park Primary School

Rainbows

Up above the sky,
Was a beautiful rainbow,
So colourful and high,
Under the arch flowers grow,
Producing fragrance every moment,
Amusing children as they pass by,
The fragrance going straight to their nose,
Filling the air with lavender and rose,
What an amazing sight in the air,
Adding lustre over the fair,
With its 7 colours shining so clear,
The children say it feels so near.

Mariyam Choudry (11)
Middleton Park Primary School

The Beast

A lonely predator, unfriendly,
Razor-like teeth, creeping in the darkness,
Blood-soaked canines, unchallenged,
Unbeatable, dwells in a cave,
Raising young, the last of its kind,
Tired but determined,
It will stop at nothing,
No one can stop it, it is the creature that will not be beaten,
It is the carnivorous being that everyone fears.

Bronze-coloured fur, scarlet red-eyes and jagged claws,
Faster than the speed of sound,
Its den is like a graveyard, full with crackling bones,
Both human and creature alike,
It has raw meat scent, blood-curling breathing,
Hatred fills its mind, like memories before,
It sees in heat-vision, and is merciless on its prey,
The fur of the creature is soaked with both blood and sweat,
The craving for blood spirals round its mind,
No one dares approach its territory or dares look at it.

The people fear for their children,
Hunters have entered its domain but few have returned,
The senses of this beast are impenetrable,
Even the breath of this creature is poisonous,
It has a great lack of energy but it is determined to breed,
But all are against it and both will fight for freedom and safety.

Adam Hepburn (12)
Middleton Park Primary School

Flowers!

Planting flowers is my hobby,
It makes me really sporty,
Flowers are cheerful, they make me laugh,
As I see them planted on the green grass,
They are red, they are purple,
They also have different colours,
I like to see flowers,
At all kinds of hours,
There is a rose, there is a violet,
There is a daisy and there is an iris,
In my garden I like to grow,
A few flowers including a rose,
One day I would love to receive,
A giant bouquet of flowers just for me!

Hajrah Ahmed (11)
Middleton Park Primary School

Colours

Colours are everywhere that I look,
You see them on TV or in your favourite book,
Pink and purple are for girls,
Up the brown branches, climbs a red squirrel,
Look up to the sunny blue sky,
That is where the white fluffy clouds lie,
I feel sad with black and grey,
I love the yellow sun on a bright summer's day,
Red and white are the colours of Aberdeen,
My dad's favourite football team,
Shiny silver and gold are the colours of money,
Black and yellow bees make the honey,
Walking through the jet-black wood,
Or across the sunny seaside,
When I'm in a happy mood,
Up and down colours everywhere,
But my favourite is the pink bow on
My fluffy teddy bear,
My brown teddy is called Sue,
Red roses on Valentine's Day,
That is the way that lovers say,
I love you.

Louise Paterson (11)
Middleton Park Primary School

Girls!

Being a girl is so much fun,
Listening to your iPod while going for a run,
Love to shop, I really must say,
Buying shoes and handbags every day.

Girls love to read their magazines in bed,
With pages of fashion in blue, pink and red,
Problem pages, celebrity goss and horoscopes,
Gives you ideas for all you can hope.

When girls are little, they like to play with toys,
But as they get older, they'd rather chat up boys!
Using their straighteners and make-up,
Are some of the signs of a girl grown-up.

So being a girl really is the best,
Especially at sleepovers when they get no rest,
So keep it girlie and pink all the way,
Girls rule! That's all I need to say!

Kendall Leigh Wright (11)
Middleton Park Primary School

My Dad

My dad works on the rigs
and he goes away a lot.
He works in India where it's always very hot.
I miss him when he goes away,
it makes me very sad,
but when he comes home he takes me fishing.
I really love my dad.

Tyler Conell Hay (11)
Middleton Park Primary School

Dinosaurs

Dinosaurs are big,
Dinosaurs are small,
But some are very tall,
Some have bony heads,
But some aren't strong at all,
Some can fly,
Some can swim,
Tyrannosaurus Rex
And Oviraptors too,
They are both meat-eaters,
I hope I don't meet one of them,
I might lose my shoe.

Kieron Haley (7)
Mill O' Forest Primary School

The Swordfish

The swordfish in the open sea,
Whizzes through the water looking for fish for tea,
If I ever caught him on a fishing rod,
I would always let him free,
When I was on a boat,
One jumped out the water with glee,
He jumps so high that he could jump over a tree,
He has enough power to fly like a bee.

Andrew Blake (7)
Mill O' Forest Primary School

If I Were A Monkey

If I were a monkey,
I would swing in the trees,
Come and join me if you please,
Bring some bananas all ready to eat.

Let's sit in that tree and have a treat,
The people below look rather sad,
Because they wanted the bananas we had.

Erin Davidson (7)
Mill O' Forest Primary School

Dogs

Big, friendly,
Very playful,
Colour black,
Floppy ears,
Circle nose,
Green eyes,
Sharp claws,
Soft bed,
Sits, begs,
Eats meat.

Gavin Gerrard (7)
New Pitsligo & St John's School

Ponies

Fast, friendly,
Likes water,
Loves people,
Having fun,
Delicious grass,
Very playful,
High, low,
Galloping fields,
Ride them,
Brush coats.

Ben Smith (8)
New Pitsligo & St John's School

Dolphin

Swimming fast,
Splashing, splishing,
Friendly creatures,
Playing, sparkly,
Shiny, jumping,
Crashing waves,
Jumping over,
Swimming school,
Underwater,
Warm sea.

Lizzie Walls (8)
New Pitsligo & St John's School

Bat

Smelly, hairy,
Big wings,
Eats fruit,
Long arms,
Night fly,
Pointed ears,
Black nose,
Tiny feet,
Shiny eyes,
Sharp claws.

Jordan McIntosh (7)
New Pitsligo & St John's School

Snake

Colour long
Scary, skinny
Sharp teeth
Slithery tongue
Tiny eyes
Poisonous, venomous
Slimy slinky
Pointed face.

Thomas McKean (7)
New Pitsligo & St John's School

Birds

Fat, brown
Eats worms
Sharp claws
Trees, bushes
Flies fast
Cats, owl
Long legged
Climbs trees
Little beaks
Big beaks
Loose feathers
Lays eggs
Little eyes
Sits quietly
Big wings
Three eyelids.

Natasha Doutre (8)
New Pitsligo & St John's School

Kangaroo

Good jumper
Long tail
Quick runner
Pointy ears
Grey skin
Very exciting
Eats grass
Sharp teeth
Spiky claws
Greedy animal
Really friendly
Skinny animals
Big mouth
Very tame
Fascinating thing
Big belly
Furry tail
Fussy eater.

Mark Forsyth (7)
New Pitsligo & St John's School

Butterfly

Caterpillar grows
Drinks nectar
Colourful wings
Likes flying
Eats leaves
Makes chrysalises
Loves spring
Swaying wings
Fly away
Back home.

Gabrielle Simpson (8)
New Pitsligo & St John's School

Elephant

Heavy animals
Likes leaves
Long tusks
Big ears
Short tails
Huge eyes
Strong trunk
Loves swimming
Patterned skin
Drinks water.

Gail Leggat (8)
New Pitsligo & St John's School

Leopards

Run fast
Have spots
Hang prey
On trees
Wild animals
Stay together
Friendly animals
Short hair
Large eyes
Pointy ears
Long legs.

Andrew McKean (9)
New Pitsligo & St John's School

Dolphins

Bottle-nosed
Endangered, beautiful
Home, Morayfirth
Fast swimmers
Fun lovers
Good leapers
Fish diet
Sweet, sensitive
Cute families
Sharp sight
Never alone
Travel close.

Fiona Park (9)
New Pitsligo & St John's School

Monkeys

Tree swingers
Slow runners
Banana eaters
Tree climbers
Cheeky faces
Big fingers
Small hands
Big feet
Bug eaters
Long arms
Skilled animals.

Ryan Chalmers (9)
New Pitsligo & St John's School

Wasp

Sinful sting
Bright yellow
Bleak stripes
Sucks nectar
Short fur
Two wings
Paper thin
Eight legs
Quite small
Big queen.

Ross Cowie (8)
New Pitsligo & St John's School

Puppies

Eater, sniffer
Cute, furry
Water fight
Playable, sleeping
Visit vet
Colourful, jumps
Whimpers, barks
Baths, sneaky
Runs, crashes
Noisy growls.

Naomi Dennis (8)
New Pitsligo & St John's School

Kittens

Litter tray
Food dishes
Scratches sore
Toys play
Bed sleeper
Stays house
Not stray
Pet carrier
Warm house
Miss mother
Two meals
A day
Dry food
Brush it
Likes milk.

Kelsey Elrick (8)
New Pitsligo & St John's School

Hamster

Eyes small
Little, slow
Fat, greedy,
Cute, cuddly,
Mischievous, fighting
Tumble around
Smelly, fast
Vegetable eater
Likes nuts
Fluffy coats.

Niall Gibbon (9)
New Pitsligo & St John's School

Dinosaur

Sharp claws
Attacks victims
Killer instinct
Big teeth
Strong jaw
Giant animal
Long tail
Eats meat
Wide mouth
Long ago.

Ben Mellin (8)
New Pitsligo & St John's School

Fear

Fear is red like blood running off my hand,
It sounds like someone screaming,
Fear reminds me of dark rooms,
It smells like horrible eggs,
Fear tastes like burnt toast,
It looks like a wolf on a hill,
Fear feels like darkness running through my bones.

Kirsty Watson (8)
Newtonhill Primary School

Anger

Anger is red like a man going mad,
Anger reminds me of someone screaming at me,
Anger feels like a bumpy road,
It looks like a red face,
It smells like smoke,
It sounds like a bomb,
Anger tastes like a hot shot.

Brodie Cooper (8)
Newtonhill Primary School

Laughter

Laughter is red like a sweet summer rose,
It looks like a funny face in the clouds,
Laughter sounds like someone telling a joke,
It smells like a big jar of strawberry jam,
Laughter feels like my heart is getting bigger,
It tastes like a jar of honey,
Laughter reminds me of my nana,
Of all the good times we had together.

Carly Bruce (8)
Newtonhill Primary School

Through My Winter Window

Snowflakes on the window,
Children going on their sledges,
Children having a snowball fight,
Through my winter window.

Youngsters going on the icy path,
Mums and dads getting the snow off the driveway,
The children ice-skating,
Through my winter window.

The snow glistening on the ground,
Children's laughter,
Footprints from animals,
Through my winter window.

Snow fights on the down,
Queues of traffic standing still,
Mums and dads sledging on the icy slopes,
Through my winter window.

Children sledging,
Squirrels in the trees,
The snowman is melting,
Through my winter window.

Robin redbreast in the snow,
Boys and girls wearing jackets and boots,
Sledging fast downhill and kids having hot chocolate,
Through my winter window.

Natalie Donald (8)
Newtonhill Primary School

Happiness

Happiness is yellow like honey,
Happiness looks like daffodils waving in the wind,
It feels like someone tickling you,
It sounds like children playing and having fun,
It reminds me of my toy boat,
Happiness tastes like sweets,
It smells like flowers.

Lewis Coyle (8)
Newtonhill Primary School

Anger

Anger is red like volcanoes,
It sounds like water bubbling,
It looks like a big mountain with red coming out,
It feels like hot water,
It smells like lemon and lime,
It tastes like burnt toast,
It reminds me of my family all together.

Saxon Thomson (8)
Newtonhill Primary School

Happiness

Happiness is yellow like the sun,
It feels like love,
Happiness sounds like Lilly, my dog barking,
It reminds me of a sunny day,
Happiness smells like the sea,
It tastes like a big ice cream,
Happiness looks like happy adults.

Abbie Crawford (8)
Newtonhill Primary School

Fear

Fear is black like darkness,
It tastes like ginger,
It sounds like screaming in the darkness,
It reminds me of a very nasty robber,
Fear feels like lightning in my tummy,
Fear looks like a volcano rumbling,
Fear smells like black smoke.

Jessica Murray (9)
Newtonhill Primary School

Through The Winter Window

Happy children having a snowball fight in the freezing cold snow,
Good friends ice-skating on the hard ice,
Cold boys and girls making a big snowman,
Through my winter window.

Gritters putting grit down on the roads,
Little boys sledging on a very steep hill,
People playing in the slush,
Through my winter window.

Men playing hockey on the icy pond,
Big dogs barking at other dogs,
Heaps of footprints everywhere,
Through my winter window.

Stewart Rennie (8)
Newtonhill Primary School

Through The Winter Window

Happy children playing outside and
Having fun hiding behind the snow towers,
Children making snowmen besides the houses,
Happy men skating on the icy lake,
Through my winter window.

Barking dogs chasing their tails,
Making circles in the snow,
Robins making footprints on the snow,
Snowflakes falling from the sky,
Through my winter window.

Rachel Bussell (8)
Newtonhill Primary School

Happiness

Happiness is blue like the sky in the morning,
It sounds like people singing in the morning,
Happiness reminds me of skipping through flowers,
It tastes like sweet honey in the morning,
Happiness smells like daffodils in a big garden,
It looks like a nice kite,
Happiness feels like a warm feeling in my stomach.

Mitchell Deighton (8)
Newtonhill Primary School

The Cat In The Tree

I can see,
A cat up a tree,
It's calling to me,
Miaow, miaow, miaow,
Someone phoned 999,
The fire brigade came rushing down,
Dashing out of town,
They put the ladder against the tree
And climbed up as quick as can be,
The cat was free.

Katie Matthew (7)
Old Rayne Primary School

Healthy Living

Happy people, happy hearts
And a person playing darts,
People running and jumping,
Exercise every day,
People doing jumping jacks and football,
You sometimes see people exercising,
Hearts are important and hearts are good.

Jed Lawson (8)
Old Rayne Primary School

Summer

S ummer is the best, nice and warm,
U nderneath the sun so bright,
M aking sandcastles which fall down,
'M ake it again,' says Mum,
E veryone joins in,
R unning round *splash* in the sea.

Mary Wilson (9)
Old Rayne Primary School

Football

F ootball is a crazy sport,
O ther people dislike it,
O nce a week we do training,
T urning, dribbling and shooting,
B lasting the ball into the net,
A t the stadium the crowd cheer,
L ots of people celebrate,
L ots of laughs all around!

Joshua Foreman (10)
Old Rayne Primary School

My Dog Morgan

M organ is my dog
O ut in the sun
R oaring at the sunflower
G oing for a run
A nd having lots of fun
N ever sad, always happy.

Kyle Dawson (8)
Old Rayne Primary School

Hamsters

Hamsters are fun,
I think they run,
I hope mine remembers,
It's his birthday in November.

Hamsters like to clean,
Even though they can be mean,
They like to jump and bite,
He might even have a sleep at night.

Emma Wood (10)
Old Rayne Primary School

Jack And Jill

Jack and Jill went to the shop,
To buy a great big lollipop,
Was Jack thinking, not at all,
Over Jill's foot he had a fall,
So Jack and Jill went to the store,
His broken leg was very sore,
On his leg was put some plaster,
How he wished he had run faster.

Cameron Baird (8)
Pitmedden School

Robbie

I have a horse called Robbie,
Looking after him is my hobby,
I put on his rug
And give him a hug,
I love my horse called Robbie.

Sarah More (8)
Pitmedden School

Brother Rory

Rory is a menace
Especially when he's playing tennis,
He rides cats down the stairs,
He throws everything from apples to pears,
I really know what Rory is like,
Sometimes he can be a tyke,
He phones 999 and he hides his food,
But in the end, his intentions are good.

Ben Pirrie (9)
Pitmedden School

My Football Boots

My football boots are all shiny
And they are red and white,
They run around and kick quite hard,
But please don't give me a yellow card.

My football boots are shiny
And they are red and white,
With grass and mud, they are a sight,
But they could make me a football star.

Ewan Grant (8)
Pitmedden School

Snakes

Snakes
Are slimy
Snakes are slimy
Snakes will make
Your dog bark.
Tiny, colourful,
They have scales
And they are
Cold
And they have
Long red
Tongues.
They are fun!
They make you
Go argh!
They will make you
Giggle,
They're great,
Long big socks
Aren't smelly
But are
Hot and warm.

Bruce Bremner (9)
Pitmedden School

Spring

Here is the spring again, the wonderful spring,
We can play in the spring again, the wonderful spring,
We can watch newborn animals in the spring,
We can look at the pretty flowers and
Watch them grow in the spring.

Ellen Forsyth (10)
Tough Primary School

The Slug

There once was a slug,
that was a big thug,
and liked to pick on snails
and other bugs with tails.
He goes round town thinking
about how to pick on snails.
At home eating the lettuce
from the house next door,
thinking about how to pick
on the other bugs with tails.

David Wood (8)
Tough Primary School

Dolphins

Dolphins are mammals,
Dolphins are nice,
Dolphins are cute,
Dolphins are fit,
Dolphins are flexible,
Dolphins are good swimmers,
Dolphins are clever,
Dolphins can speak,
You can swim with dolphins.

Steven Roberts (8)
Tough Primary School

Man United

Man United are the best team on Earth,
Man United, when they play football
I cheer for them like nothing on Earth,
I should call them 'The goal demons',
Well they do score loads of goals,
Ronaldo, Rooney, Giggs, Neville,
They are all great at football,
Football, football, nothing's better
Except Man United.

Ryan Mearns (10)
Tough Primary School

Friends

F riends are fun and cheerful,
R eally they are nice,
I don't know what I'd do without them,
E ven though they are quiet as mice,
N ever mind if they're older than me,
D oesn't make a difference,
S o as long as I've got friends - I am *happy!*

Clare Mavor (10)
Tough Primary School

Mac

Mac is my dog
And he is big,
He is lovely and cute,
But sometimes very naughty,
But I still love him,
He always runs very fast
And likes bones,
He has a patch on his eye,
He always kisses me
And likes to be on the seat with me,
But I still love him.

Emma Jayne McLeod (9)
Tough Primary School

Little Bill

There is a cat at my window waiting for some milk,
He comes every day, I call him Little Bill,
He is a tabby sort of cat and very, very cute,
My sister calls him Billy but I say *no* he is my Little Bill,
I sing little songs to him and feed him all the time,
I love Little Bill, he is my little cat.

Kerry Leanne Officer (8)
Tough Primary School

The Prime Minister's First Flight

The Prime Minister sat in his office one day,
When the window opened and he was blown away!

Past the houses and chimneys, he flew,
While the bird above him did the loo!

'Ha, you missed!' he began to cry,
Then a boy with a sling hit him in the eye!

'Oh cor, oh my, oh lumme,'
'I really want my mummy.'

Later still soaring . . .

'Oh this is boring,'
'Miss Author Ma'am can you speed things up?'
(So I decided to do something to shut him up).

So he fell . . .
Into a well . . .

The next day at a meeting they discussed how great
It would be to fly,
'Oh shut up,' snapped the Prime Minster sourly,
Nursing a black eye.

Lauren Robertson (11)
Tough Primary School

My Garden

My garden is big, it has flowers, bugs, butterflies,
It has two cheeky kittens,
They like to play about,
There's lots of nature in my garden,
Come and see it all.

Caitlyn Walker (9)
Tough Primary School

Young Writers Information

We hope you have enjoyed reading this book - and that you will continue to enjoy it in the coming years.

If you like reading and writing poetry drop us a line, or give us a call, and we'll send you a free information pack.

Alternatively if you would like to order further copies of this book or any of our other titles, then please give us a call or log onto our website at www.youngwriters.co.uk

Young Writers Information
Remus House
Coltsfoot Drive
Peterborough
PE2 9JX

(01733) 890066